For Theristes,

May Hades allow him to put down his oars
and to rest in peace.

As soon as you're born they make you feel small,
By giving you no time instead of it all,
Till the pain is so big you feel nothing at all,
A working class hero is something to be

Working Class Hero
Ozzy Osbourne

ISBN:

9780692582916

Printed in the United States of America

Second Printing

For information or to order additional books,
Please write:

Diviacchi Promotions, Inc.
Boston, MA.
617-542-3175
Or visit our website and
online catalogue at www.diviacchi.com

Sit dare vitam honestam mortem occubuisse sensum.

Son,

Do not listen to the skeptics; our 21st Century Technological Society is a great era of human history. As with all history, there is a dialectic struggle going on between the forces that want to go forward into the next era and those that want to revert or destroy history. The recent book "Between the World and Me" by Mr. Ta-Nehisi Coates exemplifies so well the bullshit used by the new economic slave masters of our Technological Society for whom he ignorantly or intentionally toils, the new Powers-that-be of all races, that serves to maintain their power at the expense of all of us trying to survive in life and most detrimentally to those whom the bullshit pretends to help. I want to use it to show you how through examination of your life experience and application of it through reason and empathy to what you read and hear, you can see through the bullshit to see the lies and to continue humanity's search for truth. I will examine Mr. Coates through the following categories he creates or uses: a) race; b) education; c) the Dream and Dreamers; d) violence; e) America, the supposed evil empire; and f) slavery. I will then give you the one undisputed empirical truth — that being poor is miserable but does not necessarily entail losing one's humanity — as well as my own categories by which I have learned to decipher bullshit from truth and lies: 1) valid *ad hominem* argument; 2) Nature including human nature is your enemy, rather than any individual person; 3) the law is not your friend; 4) morality, ethics, or any attempt to define good and evil cannot be applied to the dead; and 5) accept Despair, including religious Despair.

In most cases, the meaning of a word is its use.
    — Ludwig Wittgenstein

I.   PROLOGUE

Racism is the child of race not the father of it. In the absence of experience of physical differences between human individuals, there would be no concept of race nor racism just as in the absence of a perception of the color red, there would be no word for red, no idea of the color red, nor any preference for the use of red over other colors — "red-ism". By taking experience and categorizing it into terms and propositions — regardless of whether you call them generalizations or stereotypes — that can be used in logical thought, you are only being human and using one of Mankind's essential tools: reason. Whether terms such as "race" — or any generalization or stereotype — are sound or have any useful purpose or good intention or whether it must or should lead to irrational "racism" are substantive and important questions. None of these are asked by the majority of present-day racists of any race nor by the majority of their alleged opponents of any race. It is not about these questions that I am writing to you. As American society is becoming filled with more bullshit, run by cowards whose strongest human trait is the ability to generate and withstand bullshit, for someone who will spend most of life simply trying to survive, becoming a racist as a means of survival is easier and unfortunately a stronger temptation.

Unlike those who see the struggle as being a self-centered battle "between the world and me", despite my lifetime of solitary struggle and being an outcaste, I know it is not. I owe you a duty as my child to help you survive both in mind and body, and I have a duty as "the living, rather, to be dedicated here to the unfinished work which they who fought here, have, thus far, so nobly advanced."

The statement "black-Americans are three times more likely to die of asthma than white Americans" is not racism but a sound generalization that should not be ignored by anyone simply because it uses a race term with bad connotations in other uses. If the referenced statistical fact becomes wrong, the terms should be changed so that they accurately reflect the use but not the other way around. We can change the terms nominally to whatever we want — instead of "black" use "ghyvvd" or whatever — but the meaning will be the same. It used to be said that "sickle-cell anemia is a black disease" because based on the limited experience at the time consisting of the available statistical analysis of Americans, this appeared to be an accurate statement; it was not a racist statement at the time. Statistical experience now shows that sickle cell anemia is associated with malaria resistance. Thus, the correct non-racist generalization now would be that "sickle cell anemia is a disease of the individuals of African, Middle Eastern, Southern European, and South Asian descent in which malaria resistance outweighed the negative impact of sickle cell disease." If someone were now to say, "sickle cell anemia is a black disease", they are either good intentioned but ignorant or bad intentioned (racist) or both. None of these statements are racist or not racist in the abstract, only in their use.

One reason why important questions of pragmatics and intention are absent from public discussions on racism is because most pundits are neither smart enough nor educated enough to ask them. Another reason for these questions not being asked is because neither racists nor their supposed opponents want to ask them. Racism, as with any entitled social, ethical, or moral problem when finally taken as a serious concern by the Powers-that-be — because they see some threat there to their power — is big money to them and therefore is no longer an issue that can be rationally and honestly debated nor questioned. At best it becomes a subject of polemics in which the Powers establish the correct stance and their well-rewarded advocates and apologists march out to punish those who oppose it. Racism, as with so many -ism's, has the obvious advantage of keeping the poor arguing and fighting among themselves and thus indirectly helping the Powers concentrate on their one goal: more power. In our modern American culture of bullshit in which for the first time in history the Powers generate power directly to themselves through technological technique and the legal system, our society is full of rich and powerful white guys and gals and a separate group of rich white people who have one trait that both gained and maintains this wealth and power for them: they are black. Racism is the best thing that ever happened to them. It gives them a gift that even rich white guys who are just white do not have: wealth and power while at the same time pretending to care about the poor and powerless they left behind and leave behind by the racist polemics they are paid to spit out.

The recent book by Ta-Nehisi Coates "Between the World and Me" perfectly exemplifies the latter Powers. I want to critique it for you so you can see how deceptive pretty words on a page can be if they are not analyzed for substance and then give you my own advice on the world and us. The world is a rapidly changing place that is run by bullshit artists. Basic truths of how it operates are easy to lose in trying to survive it but must not be so lost in order to save your soul.

II. "BETWEEN THE WORLD AND ME"

I have seen this book described in many ways, probably because it says whatever those who read it want it to say and lacks any substance or cohesive rational thought or ideas — perfect bullshit. The substance of the descriptions claim it as a letter by Mr. Coates to his teenage son describing race as a necessary fabrication for a prevalent concept of American (white) identity that results in a systemized, omnipresent threat to "black bodies" derived from slavery inflicting police brutality on them. I sincerely hope his son lives the same sheltered, pampered existence that Mr. Coates seems to have lived or I pity him given the ridiculous advice that his father gives in this book. It is a perfect example of the prevalent nonsense spit out by the sycophant pundits of our times who sell themselves, either knowingly or through selfish ignorance, to the new slave masters of the 21st Century Powers to keep the lower classes arguing among themselves and thus in their proper place. It is no wonder that the curators of American (white) identity gave Mr. Coates a "genius" award for his mastery of the art of bullshit.

A.   Race

His first dogma is "race is the child of racism, not the father." This is a beautiful example of Nietzsche's description and criticism of poetry: "the art of creating ripples on shallow waters in order to give the appearance that they are deep." Such statements are truly the work of genius, especially when he goes on constantly to refer to "black bodies" in need of protection from those who call themselves "white"; of being cast into a black "race"; and of speaking the personal language of his black "people" and "tribe" whenever it is of benefit to him in his book. Not only does this statement essentially say nothing, the little it does say is completely wrong.

We live in a supposedly free country in which its supposedly free citizens are forbidden by law from discriminating on the basis of race. At the same time, the Powers, in order to be considered ethical, affirmatively hire, elect, and appoint on the basis of "race" using an excuse called "diversity": even though the appointees who are hired or elected are just as pro-mass incarceration, pro-corporation, pro-prosecution, pro-big business, pro-Wall Street, and pro-war, and just as willing to use secret drones to kill people as any white dude in the same job would have done and thus add no diversity. Some day we might live in a uni-sex and uni-skin color world in which terms such as sex and race are meaningless (according to Mr. Coates, such a "beige" world would not alter its nature anyway), until then use your rational mind and its experience to see the world as it is not only so you survive it but so that you work to will it to be something else. According to Mr. Coates, he and the persons he approves can use the terms "black bodies", "race", and "tribes" when it benefits them, but everyone else are or should be — he is not clear which — raceless. Such hypocritical arguments that attempt to separate the meanings of words from their use to create an independent abstract reality of, for, and by bullshit supports, creates, and incites racism, they are not arguments against it.

B.   Education

This one is personal. (I will get into why it is sound and valid to take and make criticism personal; *ad hominem* argument is sound and valid when used properly.)   In the absence of pure, dumb luck, education is the only legal way that poor kids have of not remaining poor — even with it, the odds are against them.

As the son of two illiterate parents and the first in his family to graduate from high school and college, I perceive Mr. Coates as coming from a highly educated, prosperous, comfortable, and even prestigious family. Even from the perspective of the average person, he comes from a flourishing family. His parents (plus at least one if not all of his grandparents), siblings, and close relatives were college educated. His mother was a teacher. His father not only published and wrote books but eventually became a university librarian at the "Mecca" of Howard University. If he did not go to private school, Mr. Coates must have gone to an excellent or special public school since he complains of being forced to take "seventh grade French". "Seventh grade French"! WTF? In my neighborhood, until maybe high school if you did not drop out, the only foreign language experience we received was the language you spoke at home after finishing your English classes in school. After graduating from high school, he went on to college for five years but he failed to graduate. Apparently this genius was the first in his family not to graduate from college, though he wasted five years, a lot of his family's money, and Howard University's financial assistance, that could have gone to someone who really wanted and needed it, trying to complete what has become a relatively simple task if you can afford the tuition. Despite this failure to graduate, he is well versed enough in the workings of academia to attend some type of graduate program in French at Middlebury College so that he can attend a "fellowship" in Paris to admire how wide French doors are, sit in cafes, and walk the streets of Paris, laughing from afar at the American *bourgeoisie* and *hoi polloi* and thus following the worst traditions of the French intelligentsia. While doing so, he apparently was and is completely ignorant of the fact that he was only able to do so because many of those *hoi polloi* died to free Paris from the Nazis, the last major Western proponents of slavery and racism, while that same intelligentsia were doing the same then as they do now: sitting in cafes, walking Paris, and laughing at Americans only at that time they did it with the Nazis instead of the present politically correct "black bodies".

Mr. Coates is educated enough to know that "[f]ully 60 percent of all young black men who drop out of high school will go to jail." As society gets more complex and even the simplest of tasks require more education, this statistic will likely worsen. Even the conservative, narrow American formal education that he has completed when added to his genius for bullshit has given Mr. Coates money and power and he should be nothing by grateful to the educational system that has given them to him. Instead, knowing what he does about what happens to drop-outs, what does he do? He ridicules it. Mr. Coates thinks school is "only an opportunity to discipline the body", that involves "writing between the lines", "copying the directions legibly", and "memorizing theorems". He writes "[t]hey were concerned with compliance" and "Algebra, Biology, English" are just excuses for "discipline." What an asshole. If Mr. Coates thinks schools are boring, authoritarian, uncaring, and only concerned that students follow orders and generate a profit for the school, then Mr. Coates should try work, the type of work that he has apparently spent a lifetime either avoiding or failing to accomplish but that provides the bread and butter for the vast majority of the rest of the world, both the working and middle classes. Work in which you are expected to show up on time, spend your day at whatever tedious task your employer orders you to do that day, wait until you are allowed to leave, go home, and then come back the next day to repeat the cycle again.

Maybe someday our world will survive with a completely self-centered educational system in which everyone can spend their days fucking around and reading and writing only about themselves or about whatever they want and whenever they want as Mr. Coates apparently did but I do not see it happening in the near future. Until then, at a minimum, an education system has a duty to all the poor and most of the middle class to teach them physical and mental discipline. With this plus a lot of luck, if they can add ambition, intelligence, and creativity, they have a hope of working their way out of being poor or middle class, whether legally or illegally — even being a successful criminal requires discipline. In many ways, I would have been better educated had I been given a library card at age seven and then left alone in it for the next 11 years — a better education but most likely dead. Being forced to discipline oneself to follow directions, appear on time and where one is told, and to concentrate on simple tasks for long periods of time is basic survival for the poor. If you are not "educated" enough in such basic self discipline, you will not survive as poor but will go either to jail where the jailers will provide you with this education in discipline or to homelessness and an early death. If a poor person cannot force themselves to show up to school on time; do whatever work is assigned regardless of how boring or tedious it may appear; comply with deadlines; follow directions; and memorize as necessary, they are screwed. Instead of just being poor, most likely their future is prison in which the jailers will provide the physical and mental discipline they missed in school.

Education and working for a living used to be and should be a source of pride in itself that has and will continue to contribute to civilization and that should be rewarded and commended by society, regardless of whether the work is physical or involves being stuck in a cubicle.

What alternative does Mr. Coates give? According to him, at age four, one should start to ignore school and have their mother and grandmother teach one how to read and write and then you start writing essays about "me", my problems, my sense of injustice, and how I feel about "me." At that point, you should start reading the books that one's parents want one to read, which for Mr. Coates appeared to be the Black Panther writings published by his Dad and the great Malcolm X. This need and motivation to read books about "black bodies" and "me" should continue through college and beyond. Students should not be forced to memorize "theorems extracted from the world they were created to represent" but theorems extracted from his or one's parents' self-centered imagination created to further boast one's ego. Apparently, it is not acceptable to study turning points in history varying from the Battle of Salamis to the Battle of Stalingrad; from the rejection of purely religious techniques for the study of reality to the rational study of it including the creation of formal logical systems and of the scientific method; from Aristotelian physics to classical and quantum and relativity physics; and from the Roman and Greek worship of the state to the history of Christianity and its "Slave Morality" without which slavery would still be an acceptable norm in the world. According to Mr. Coates, all of the latter raceless subjects must be rejected as racist American (white) identity.

Is this a formula for success? It seems to have worked for Mr. Coates in the lucky circumstances of his flourishing family so that he could wait until college to drop out, but I do not see how it would work for the typical high school drop out. It certainly did not work for Malcolm X. His preaching of how to beat the Powers did not work for him and have not worked for anyone since. The Powers put him in jail for a large part of his life, for stupid shit like larceny. When he finally got out and started earning an honest living, he was shot by his fellow "black bodies" — either because they did not like what he was saying while having no respect for the American ideal of freedom of speech or because he was fucking too many of their wives and girlfriends or for both reasons. Malcolm X was essentially an orphan and, unlike Mr. Coates, came from a very dysfunctional family and personal background. So, as far as I am concerned, he had a valid excuse for his advocating of an alternative doomed to failure. Why does Mr. Coates propose it despite having received nothing but opportunity from the American educational system?

If he had been more liberal and open-minded in his studies, Mr. Coates might have learned "for the hand that rocks the cradle, is the hand that rules the world." Regardless of how well the propaganda may be spread in an educational system, they are still handicapped by the need to brainwash 30 to 40 students at a time in one class. Mothers or fathers have the benefit of concentrating their propaganda and brainwashing at one child, one student, at a time — especially one that considers himself or herself loved and therefore has no reason to repel or oppose the parental propaganda. Mr. Coates gives his alternative because it is how he was educated, he does not have the imagination or empathy to understand any other method.

Mr. Coates is not giving "black bodies" an alternative to the educational system but an excuse for failing it: past slavery. It is really beyond me why he uses it as such instead of using it as a source of pride and incentive for American "black bodies", as most working class people use adversities in their history. The more this excuse is used, the more books he seems to sell. His alternative to having "black bodies" suffer through a tedious educational system like the rest of us must do in order to survive in life is an argument for racism not against it.

C.   The "Dream" and "Dreamers."

Mr. Coates's family background is such that they could have lived in a nice suburb either with the white "Dreamers" or in areas such as Prince George's County with the other "black bodies" living the "Dream" that he complains is unobtainable by "black bodies". Instead, his family and now he freely choose and chose not do live it or by their chosen life style rejected the financial discipline required to achieve it. Mr. Coates' father, a former Black Panther, had seven children by four women, who apparently did not believe in monogamy but in the free love preached by the Black Panthers. Apparently, his dream life did not involve living a parochial, suburban life with one wife and working his whole life to maintain that life. Fine, whatever. However, this situation is substantively different on all levels from not having the choice to live the Dream at all and Mr. Coates should stop pretending that neither he nor his family ever had the choice to live the Dream or that he understands what it is like never to have had the choice to live the "Dream." Mr. Coates now lives in Harlem because he wants do live there, not because he has to live there. As with his ridiculing of education, he is again taking away one of the few "Dreams" that the poor have to stop being poor. He is an asshole for doing this. Life will soon enough take away the poor's Dreams and kill their Dreamers. They do not need tourists to their lot in life such as Mr. Coates doing it also.

Mr. Coates spends a lot of his time talking about how he lived in "fear" while growing up in a crime-infested, violence infested, drug infested, and physically and mentally numbing part of Baltimore. However, most his descriptions are of what he witnessed happening to others or what others told him was happening. The only violence that he describes as actually being inflicted upon him was by his father. Apparently, since he beat Mr. Coates as a child for allowing someone to steal from him instead of beating the person who did the stealing, as would normally occur in a white or black working class family, his father wanted Mr. Coates to grow up to become a violent man as he was (and was successful in this goal in some ways as I will discuss later). Yet, he ends this depressing description of life in Baltimore by saying that "I did love Baltimore. ... I always thought that I was destined to go back home after college — but not simply because I loved home but because I could not imagine much else for myself. And that stunted imagination is something I owe to my chains." WTF?

I wanted to get away from my neighborhood and its hopelessness so badly that I joined the fuckin Navy and have worked hard the rest of my life afterward to never go back to where I came from. According to Mr. Coates, he was a sensitive child so filled with curiosity that he felt the schools he was forced to attend were boring and irrelevant. He supposedly was a bright, sensitive, creative child, yet the best he could imagine for life was fuckin loser Baltimore? What chains? The only chains that I see are mental and consist of brainwashing by his asshole father, who filled him with so much racial hatred of the white race that he excuses the only violence that he personally suffered in his childhood: family violence.

Again, what does Mr. Coates propose as an alternative to the Dream and the Dreamers? He spends the remainder of the book going in circles and ranting contradictorily and usually incoherently from "race is the child of racism not the father" to "[y]ou have been cast into a race" that needs to protect the "black body" to complaining of those who make or believe themselves to be "white" or "black", though we are all of the same humanity, to complaining about "dullards" who believe all should be the same "race" and other versions of this same ranting. As best as I can figure it out, his substantive advice to his son appears to be: "Dude, life sucks, humans spend their lives struggling in misery and fear and then you die motherfucker and then there is nothing, get used to it." Except for the fear part, I see this as sound advice if you truly see the world as a struggle between the world and "me". If his son is strong enough to accept this advice, it could be a true emancipation of his will. Life is all you got, so live it to the fullest. Ignore what others say or any obligations — moral, ethical, social, or whatever — "they", that is those white people with their nonsense identity of American excellence, want to put on you because in the end all of it is a false Dream and the Dreamers are simply out to kill you so that they can enjoy life to their fullest at your expense.

Live the life of the true existentialist if not a nihilist? If this is his advice, then why all the whining about slavery? With or without slavery, life will still suck and then we still die into nothingness. Is it because slavery gives his son an excuse for failure and for any harm he does to others who may also be trying to live life, but so what? Failure matters if winning matters. According to Mr. Coates, neither matters.

Mr. Coates has no clue as to what he is saying, nor is he giving any alternative to the Dream or the Dreamers, nor is he even capable of coming up with an alternative, nor does he want one. In my neighborhood, Mr. Coates, with college-educated siblings, as the son of college educated parents, one who was a teacher and the other a writer and book publisher and then a librarian, would have been a big fish in a small pond, the king of our parochial hill. No doubt, if his description of his neighborhood is in anyway true, he was the king of the hill and big fish among his peers. Except for his father, Mr. Coates was the one dishing out the power of violence as his father wanted him to do and not the target of it. He remained king until he left his small pond and realized that the world did not give a rat's ass who he was or who he thought he was. He then realized the way to get back on top of the hill was to pretend to be a new James Baldwin; more specifically, the James Baldwin whom the American white intelligentsia want, one that destroys the Dream and the Dreamers while providing no replacement for them. Ensuring racism continues and that slavery is an excuse for all failures by "black bodies" is not only his bread and butter, without need of rational support, but serves the purpose of the Powers who pay him. If Mr. Coates is really the new James Baldwin, this would be an argument for racism not against it.

D.   Violence

Except for his intra-family violence, such as his father beating him, according to Mr. Coates' story, he has no personal experience being the victim of violence yet does nothing but irrationally obsess about it and fears it in a way that I have only seen among suburban soccer moms. His one story of violence that personally involved him occurred when he "adopted the rules of the street ... [w]henever it was me on top of someone, whatever my rage at the moment, afterward I always felt sick at having lowered to the crudest form of communication". His father's attempts to turn Mr. Coates into a violent man like he was apparently worked for Mr. Coates' childhood years in Baltimore — he appears to have been a bully but now regrets it. I assume he also regrets threatening his ninth-grade teacher. This is understandable, admitting to being a bully not only with your fellow students but with a teacher trying to educate you and writing about how much fun it was would not sell any books. (How much of this regret is due to another bully or one of his victims showing Mr. Coates a gun and his realizing that this bullying may in fact work both ways is an open issue.) As bad as he may feel, I tell you as someone who was always on the bottom of getting beaten by the "rage of the moment", the people on the receiving end of his rage were much sicker and, until they learn to fight back against the likes of Mr. Coates and his father, would remain much sicker and more in fear of violence than he could imagine. If he could imagine it, he would have more empathy for the "meek" inheriting the earth instead of ridiculing it.

Mr. Coates' remaining descriptions of violence are his supposed witnessing of threats of violence by others against others and secondhand and even more further removed supposed descriptions of what may or may not have happened. He has no personal experience with police violence — either as a victim or witness. The one police encounter he describes consists of a traffic stop in which police shined flashlights at him, viewed his license, and then let him go with no arrest, ticket, warning, or anything yet he was in "fear" of them. Sounds like a great stop to me and better than most that I have had with police. He has never been arrested nor done jail time. By his comment about prisoners being raped in the local county jail, he admits to not knowing anyone who actually has been in jail but instead relies on stereotypes that he has heard about prison inmates.

He claims familiarity with the "rules of the street" but I doubt it. A basic rule of the street is that if you are going to pull an Eric Garner, Marlene Pinnock, Elmer Clay Newman, Gary Hopkins, Jr., or Freddie McCollum and pick a fight with someone carrying a gun, especially a cop carrying a gun who may be having a bad day dealing with other tough guys (or gals these days) who wanted to pick fights with cops, you have two options to successfully survive that fight unharmed: kill the motherfucker; or be good and quick enough to get away. If neither, either shut up and cuff up or accept the consequences like a man and stop whining about the predictable result — either a beating or killing that will most certainly occur. It is also basic street sense that if you are going to pull a Renisha McBride, John Crawford, or Tamir Rice and go around stores or parks carrying a fake gun and pointing it at people or into their redneck neighborhoods knocking on their doors and windows in the middle of the night, make sure none of those dumb hicks have a gun anywhere near by. Those idiots routinely shoot their own children, fathers, mothers, brothers, sisters, and wives with the guns they love to carry and shoot, they will not think twice about killing your dumb ass.

Reality is not television, not even reality television. In the real world, people including cops are afraid of dying. Thinking that the police are here to help you or that violence will stop by simply putting up your hands or saying "I can't breathe" when clearly you can breathe since you are saying "I can't" is how suburban fucks with no sense of street rules look at the world. Mr. Coates apparently looks at the world that way, his claim to street knowledge is just more of his bullshit.

Perhaps his "fear" of violence is not based on personal experience but with facts and statistical figures that he knows and fails to mention in his book. This makes even less sense. Police being police, they do not keep accurate records on the number of people they kill. Thus the available statistics for the last few years vary from an average of 63/year to as high as 602/year. The majority killed are white (whites are twice as likely to be killed by police officers which makes no sense given Mr. Coates' criticism because blacks and whites commit roughly an equal number of crimes.) It might be a reasonable assumption that most were not murdered but their deaths were legally justifiable in some way; but, since it is not clear on what Mr. Coates is basing his fear, I will assume as true the higher figure of 602, that they were all murders, and that all of the victims were black. Based on these assumptions, police are murdering 603 "black bodies" a year. During the last few years, there were approximately 10,000 to 14,000 murders a year. Sadly, most of these murders have gone unsolved. The exact numbers are unclear because large urban areas such as Chicago, New York City, and even Gary, Indiana, have stopped reporting their homicide arrests to FBI statisticians, apparently out of embarrassment. In a good year, an urban area such as the city of Boston solves about 45% of its murders. In a bad year (2012), Detroit solved only 9% (34 out of 386) and New Orleans solved only 15 out of its 193 killings in 2012. Of the number of solved murders in the past few years, the low-end average of male "black bodies" killed by other male "black bodies" is about 2250. (Similarly, most white victims are killed by other whites, apparently human nature likes to kill its own kind before they go on to others.) So, Mr. Coates is three times more likely to be killed by a brother member of his "race", "tribe", or whatever he wants to call himself at his convenience than he is by police. (The chances would be higher by a large multiple if we used honest assumptions).

Yet, he writes no book about his "fear" of his fellow "black bodies". In fact, he writes that blacks forgive "black on black" violence because of past slavery and when he meets other "black bodies" at airports, they knowingly glance at each other and know they share a special bond. What gives? Does he have some kind of special hand signal that makes him immune from black-on-black murder and thus has no fear? If so, he should pass it along to the rest of his "tribe". If he does not fear this higher probability of violence, why does he fear the almost zero chance of violence from the police? If both are caused by slavery, why is the solution to one excuse and forgiveness for the violent, but for the other it requires punishment, prison, monetary penalties, and accountability for the violent?

He makes even less sense when he pretends to deal with specific cases such as Prince Jones, Jr. who appears to have had a similar life to Mr. Coates except the Jones family choose to live the Dream instead of rejecting it for a life of free love. He was handsome, friendly, and always a perfect Southern gentlemen, and thus everyone loved him, including Mr. Coates. He appeared to have been a typical, upper-middle-class, spoiled, sheltered, suburban, trust fund kid who spent seven years in college (Howard University) without graduating because he was trying to "find himself". While unable to find himself, he was able to find a baby mama with whom he worked out his domestic abuse issues — such as kicking and punching this pregnant girlfriend when she was eight months pregnant — and found time to father a child. Despite such failures, according to Mr. Coates, all black-bodies who met Mr. Jones agreed with the obvious conclusion that he had great potential in life, because unlike so many *hoi polloi*, he had money, looks, and a great personality, and came from a fine, upstanding, socially respected family — what else would one need to be a success in life? Unfortunately, one of the things he lacked was common sense that when combined with his sheltered life and arrogant, self-centered view of himself and the world, gave him the brilliant idea to ram his Jeep, that his mommy bought him, into a police car because, as with Mr. Coates, he was highly sensitive to having unwanted contact with peasants such as the police.

Because Mr. Prince could not satisfy the two options stated above for picking a fight with a cop, the incident ended with the cop killing him. Mr. Coates and the Jones family demanded justice. By that, they meant that the police officer be tried, convicted, and sent to jail for murder and civil rights violations because he is obviously a racist, and the county employer pay serious money in damages and change its racist hiring and training practices and known history of police brutality to "black bodies". What Mr. Coates leaves out of his analysis and conclusion that this killing results from systemic racism and was derived from slavery is that the black victim was killed by a black cop from a black county — Prince George's County, Maryland.

So how does this analysis go? According to Mr. Coates, "black bodies" because there was slavery in the past accept and forgive violence by other "black bodies" including violence on "black bodies"; accept and forgive irresponsibility by black men as fathers; and accept and forgive drop-out black students. Ergo, the police are racist, even if the police are black. There seem to be missing premises here that I do not see. Why does this forgiveness not apply to the black cop who shot Mr. Jones nor to the black county that employed and trained him? Is slavery only an excuse for "black bodies" that are acceptable to Mr. Coates and cops are not acceptable because they made a traffic stop of him once? Is Mr. Coates saying that counties made up of black voters and administrators should know better than to hire a black man as a cop because due to past slavery he will be irresponsible, not susceptible to education and training, and is destined to commit violence. Isn't that racist? Or, is he saying that it is racist to have a county run by black administrators because they are doomed to the same flaws of irresponsibility, violence, and ignorance because of past slavery? Isn't that racist?

What about the jury made up almost evenly of Prince George's County white and black residents who found negligence by the cop and by Mr. Jones in contributing to his death? Were the white jurors racist but not the black jurors? Were they racist because they did not believe the cop's story that he feared for his life or because they did believe it? Is this a class thing? The cop Carlton Jones was a Dreamer trying to work his way up to the Dream by becoming a police officer and joining the Army Reserve, thus giving diversity to both; he did not bum around for 5 - 7 years in college trying to find himself. No, that can't be it. If race does not exist as Mr. Coates says, it cannot be that "class" exists and he simply has contempt for the lower class cop who obviously was beneath the dignity of a Mr. Jones?

As with everything else, Mr. Coates has no clue as to what he is saying other than to spit out to his readers what they want to hear. More likely, he plays on the very stereotypes about which he complains — that black men have suffered violent lives — to establish his credibility as a "black body" and gain sympathy from the clueless American intelligentsia audience to whom he is pandering. More importantly, as with his other complaints, he gives no alternative to the alleged problem of the systemic police brutality he irrationally fears other than generic whining that police should not be meanies. This is especially true when one considers his concern for unconstitutional stops of black men but gives no concern to the thousands of unsolved murders of black men by black men. If any self-respecting wealthy suburb had anywhere near an equivalent amount of unsolved murders, even a fraction of it, as demonstrated by the recent Boston Marathon and 9/11 bombings but also going back to the multiple Sedition Acts of our American history, no one would give a fuck about the Constitution. In such situation, we would have thousands of police with millions of dollars of equipment earning millions of dollars in overtime forcibly closing and searching every neighborhood in anyway related to the murders and anywhere near the suburb until the perpetrators were caught.

The honest truth is that we accept unsolved murders of the poor, both black and white, as the price to be paid for the constitutional protections about which Mr. Coates, along with suburban soccer moms and the American intelligentsia (black and white), is most concerned and most in "fear" of losing and for which he and they are willing to pay with the poor's lives — but not his or theirs of course. His irrational fear of the police but forgiving view of what will certainly be forever unsolved murders of "black bodies" by "black bodies" is an argument for racism not against it.

E. America, the Supposed Evil Empire

Mr. Coates derides America, "whose armies fanned out across the world to extend their dominion". Again, beautiful poetry such as this is either an intentional lie or the stuff of ignorant writers who spent their school years reading about themselves and neither read nor were able to imagine any other history or problems other than their own lives. If America's military has spent the 225 years of its history fanning out across the world to extend its dominion, it has been a complete failure at it. For four years between August 1945 and August 1949, the United States was the only military in the world that possessed nuclear bombs. Try saying that with some other states and then think how history may have been different or even if there would be any history: in its time, the Roman Army was the only military in the world that possessed nuclear bombs; in its time, the Ming Dynasty was the only military in the world that possessed nuclear bombs; in his time, Genghis Khan had the only military in the world that possessed nuclear bombs; Stalinist Russia was the only military in the world that possessed nuclear bombs; Maoist China was the only military in the world that possessed nuclear bombs; or as the simplest example, apply this idea to our enemies at the time consisting of the Empire of Japan and the Third Reich. If you want to see armies extending dominion over conquered lands, you should stop complaining about how boring school is, spend some time in the school library, and start reading and thinking about the lives of persons other than oneself or related to oneself through histories of the many true military empires of the past.

Contemplating the military history of the United States causes Despair not because of its failed plans to fan out "across the world to extend their dominion" but because despite the exact opposite hopes and intentions, the results have been such that it might as well have had such plans and might have been better off if it had. We had four years to do what we wanted with the world. We could have used our nuclear weapons to try to start a *Pax Americana,* an updated version of the *Pax Romana* that started the Christian Era or the *Pax Britannia* that started the Industrial Era; instead we tried to do it with the Marshall Plan of lending money to our defeated foes and not requiring much of the debt be paid back. The dispute as to which was the better choice will be left to historians a thousand years from now, if we are still around. We picked the Marshall Plan due to our corruption by "Slave Morality" that at least at that time defeated the "Master Morality" of our foe.

I met a lot of perverts, scum, and low-lifes in the military but I also met probably the most honest, dependable, and trustworthy men with whom I have ever dealt. I spent six years in the military essentially giving the government a blank check for my life, to use or lose as it pleased. I did this for the same reason everyone else did — we wanted to get the hell out of whatever loser situation in which we were stuck;

36

wanted to get education and training; wanted to prove our manhood; and serve our country while doing so. When I enlisted, neither I nor anyone I had ever met or read about who joined the United States Military either by draft or enlistment made a *sacramentum militare* to faithfully execute the commands of the emperor. The oath we took was to defend the Constitution, which Mr. Coates is always preaching about protecting as long as it does not involve risk for him. Unfortunately, the Powers and their commissioned officers used our naivete and unfortunate circumstances to inflict their agenda of power, not with the efficiency of a Roman, Spartan, or Athenian military by being honest about what they were doing, but by inefficiently hiding behind Christian principles that they routinely violated — as the Powers-that-be always take advantage of the less fortunate and always will. This fact of life does not negate the "good intentions" of the American military as Mr. Coates dogmatically states, which I will discuss later.

F.   Slavery

Mr. Coates has even less experience and knowledge about slavery though as a racist he assumes as dogma that because he is black he must know what slavery was, is, and causes. The word "slave" derives from "Slav", the word used by much of Europe for the peoples of the Balkans who endured centuries of slavery at the hands of African and Eastern Muslim conquerors (and the Romans and Byzantines before that). Mr. Coates complains about and bases the credibility of his complaints upon 250 years of slavery for his "black bodies" in the United States (yet he does not seem to complain about the several millennia of it in Africa). My Croatian ancestors have that 250 beat by another 1500 years, so does that give me eight times more credibility? Or, since I am white, I have no credibility on this issue because of my race in his analysis spitting out that "race is the child of racism"? If so, is he the racist?

Slavery as he uses that term was never "criminal" as he calls it. It was the exact opposite. As with tort, contract, constitutional, tax, and many other areas of the "law", slavery was an area of law establishing and administering obligations and duties for all involved: the state, the owner, and the slave. American slaves as with all slaves throughout both Old and New Worlds including so called "Native" America nations for millennia were not in "chains" bolted to a jailhouse wall watched over by guards. They were chained to their master by the majesty of the law. They were born, lived, worked, studied, enjoyed and despaired in it, had hopes and fears, and procreated as all humans have done throughout history but with the additional dream of being legally free. They did so as part of an accepted normative social structure and organization. Many through the legal system eventually earned their freedom and then went on to buy their own slaves. Though some ancient philosophers opposed slavery as a social norm such as Alcidamas and Euripides and even some ancient politicians opposed it, they were rare. Until Christianity developed as a dominant part of Western Civilization with its "Slave Morality", there was no normative basis to oppose slavery as a rule of law — there still is none.

The abolitionists who risked life and property and who died fighting against slavery were the criminals under the law and they were often punished as criminals, including by execution. According to Mr. Coates, such good intentions are meaningless in the infinite span of time/space and their lives do nothing to diminish his fear that someone is out to get him. As valuable property, slaves were protected under the law as any valuable property would be protected and often better than the free. Being the efficient assholes that the Powers usually are, the insurers of the American slave ships kept accurate records of their valuable cargo and the means of transporting it; thus from the records we know that the unfortunate, enslaved souls died at a rate of 83 per 1,000 during this notorious Middle Passage. These records also show that the unfortunate, legally "free" ship's crews of this notorious Passage suffered death rates of 230 per 1,000. So, based on a strict rational choice theory of human action, if the primary concern is to survive the Middle Passage, you were better off traveling it in the slavehold then as part of the ship's crew.

Those in economic slavery, that continues to this day and is becoming the norm, often had no better quality of life than those enslaved by law and often it was worse. This became more true after the British Empire and then America abolished the slave trade in 1807-08 and militarily enforced this abolition by the British West Africa Fleet against the African kings who wanted it to continue. Again, of course, the lives of the thousands of British sailors who died in that Fleet mean nothing to diminish Mr. Coate's fear of the world. At that point, American slaves were very valuable property, in fact were the equivalent of money to the South since they could not be replaced, and the South had every legal and economic incentive to feed, house, and care for them as best they could. This was not true of the 35,000 a year industrial workers, miners, and construction laborers who died on average in Northern factories during the Industrial Revolution, in mines throughout the country, and in the massive 19th Century nationwide construction projects. Nor of the millions that were injured alongside them without at that time any legal right for disability compensation or tort liability. There were plenty of desperate "free" immigrants around to replace them and thus they were treated as expendable, not valuable, commodities.

As I said before, I do not understand why Mr. Coates would not use slavery as a source of pride and incentive for education and hope as every other former slave peoples do instead of as an excuse. According to those same insurance records, about 400,000 to 500,000 African slaves, about 3% - 6% of the Atlantic African slave trade, were brought to the United States before the trade was abolished in 1808. (We will ignore the slaves from Russian and the Balkans brought to the Americas since everyone ignores them anyway and the free Africans that came here as conquistadores or settlers.) The remainder primarily went to the Carribean and South America. Mr. Coates' complains should be written in Spanish or Portuguese but their former colonies seem to have bigger problems that political correctness and most likely would not waste money on his B.S. anyway. Despite the hardships they faced, relative to world history, they not only survived but prospered. In 250 years, they got their freedom. It took Balkan and Russian slaves multiple millennia to achieve freedom and Middle Eastern slaves until the 1960's. I would argue that because of communism, the Russian slave-and-serf mentality still has not achieved freedom. The descendants of those 400,000 to 500,000 propagated to 4,000,000 by 1860 and to maybe 40,000,000 by today (It is unclear as to what percentage are post-slavery immigrants). This is an amazing triumph. Much of slavery throughout history resulted in a genocide of the enslaved or at least in a ravaging reduction of their population.

If you want to read about Man's inhumanity to Man, a better reading than American slavery would be studying the Roman Republic's final solution to the Carthage problem or its punishment and suppression of the slave rebellion led by Spartacus; the genocide of Melos by the Athenian Empire; any of the military campaigns of Genghis Khan's Mongols against China or the Middle East; the Battle of Stalingrad (actually, read about the Eastern Front Campaign in which more people died that all of the wars of Western History combined); or the Rape of Nanking, just as light reading starters. In fact, Mr. Coates should read about his and his son's namesakes and all of the great African warriors who used and use 12 year old "free" boys as front line troops. Even better, read about his hero Malcolm X's favorite religion Islam's unique military strategy of using slaves, including captured boys whom it had orphaned in prior campaigns to indoctrinate and train them from an early age, as front line troops promising them freedom if they won enough battles. (The last one is unique to Islam because it usually backfired; the boy slaves once they grew and were battle hardened had a tendency to turn around, kill their masters, and then become the new masters until the cycle repeated with the slave troops they created.) If lynching bothers you, try reading about the use of impalement as a punishment by both the Byzantine Empire and its opponents the Ottoman Empire. He is frightened by American ghettos, badly designed public housing, and red-lining — the bank lending practice of not allowing mortgages for every neighborhood in which one wants to buy a house, but only some of them. Is he serious? I suggest he read about the history of the term "ghetto" and visit the private shanties of the "free" around Rio De Janeiro or Lagos to see what kind of mortgage he can get for that property. American slave owners were amateurs in brutality when compared to the Powers of the Old World and little worse, if not better, than the capitalists of the North.

So how did this slavery omnipresent throughout history cause an alleged present systemized, omnipresent threat to "black bodies" educed from slavery inflicting upon them police brutality that would not have occurred in its absence — that is through the normal brutality of the Powers upon the "free"? Mr. Coates does not say, it is just assumed as another one of his dogmas. Is his theory that because most if not all living humans are descendants of slaves, we have poverty and violence in the world? Interesting theory. He could be right. Now that most of the world is eliminating the legal concept of slavery, should we dream of a world free of poverty and violence? Mr. Coates says no, Dreamers and Dreams suck and should be feared. So, that is not it. Well, what is it?

Clearly, slavery did not and does not affect him or his family individually in this way. In just two or three generations, his family went from beings slaves to being college educated, flourishing individuals with the power to ridicule the Dream and Dreamers. My family — as far back as anyone remembers and probably centuries earlier — consists of uneducated, illiterate, peasants engaged in subsistence farming whose life routine of working and finally dying with at best a name but no elegy written in a country churchyard was only interrupted by war. My great grandfather was conscripted by the Austro-Hungarian Empire to fight the Italians; my grandfather was conscripted by the Italians to fight the Austro-Hungarian Empire; the Nazis did not bother with conscription, they just took men to slave labor camps leaving the women and children to work the farms as a form of old school feminism; the communists conscripted my father to fight the United States; and then I was so conned by the delusions of the United States that I volunteered to fight and die if need be to stop the communists.

What a joke. If slavery only delays a family's flourishing for two or three generations, relatively speaking on the global scale of injustice, things could have been much worse for Mr. Coates given that he states he would have been more of an African queen's human leg cushion than African royalty. Being the descendant of American slaves seems to be the best thing that ever happened to him. Otherwise, he would be just another college drop-out white dude trying to avoid a life of cubicles by becoming a writer with nothing really to write about or some African queen's human leg cushion.

So, if slavery has only affected Mr. Coates for the better, how about the rest of the "black bodies"? He is unclear, but he appears to be referencing not the fact that some black bodies are uneducated, poor, and violent but that they are disproportionally uneducated,

45

poor, and violent. Since almost everyone is a descendant of a slave, to say that slavery causes uneducated, poor, and violent descendants is pragmatically meaningless at this point in history and would add nothing to Mr. Coates' thesis; if this were his argument, everyone could use slavery as an excuse for their problems — even the cops that he fears.

His argument appears to be that because black bodies are the most recently freed slaves, slavery is the cause of their disproportion in education, poverty, and violence. Among racial and ethnic groups, people calling themselves black:

— have the highest poverty rate, 27.4%, with whites at 9.9%;

— though they make up only 13% of the American population, from 2011 to 2013, 38.5 per cent of people arrested for murder, manslaughter, rape, robbery, and aggravated assault were black. Though there is a 13% black population, black males aged 15-34 account for only around 3% of the population but are responsible for the majority of these crimes.

— Despite being outnumbered by whites five to one, blacks commit eight times more crimes against whites than vice-versa, according to FBI statistics from 2007. A black male is 40 times as likely to assault a white person as the reverse. These figures also show that interracial rape is almost exclusively black on white.

(Mr. Coates better not complain that these figures should be "raceless". If he wants to measure all of these records as simply issues of the poor and uneducated classes, he should say so and stop writing books complaining about American white identity and how it brutalizes black bodies.)

He may be right about this, American blacks were the last large group of people freed in the United States. There are others groups in other parts of the world that were not freed until much later. Some Islamic states did not free their slaves until recently, such as Saudi Arabia in 1962, Oman in 1970, and Mauritania in 2007. Being the genius that he is, Mr. Coates could engage in an empirical study to compare the social state of earlier freed slaves to later ones in order to see if there are any statistical correlations and thus test his theory. Nah, no reason to get facts in the way of polemics.

Let's assume he is right, which he may be, so what do we do about it? According to him, it is racist to force black bodies through the same educational system as whites — all that boring discipline, theorems from reality, world history, and so forth forced into arbitrary time periods such as college graduation within four years. We apparently need to give them a completely separate but equal education system in which I guess they will study the failed theorems spit out by Malcolm X, esoteric African history, Swahili in the seventh grade, and whatever Mr. Coates thinks is relevant to his world view and then give them as much time as they need to complete the curriculum of Coates' dogma — no reason to discipline them with such matters as standing in line, following directions, or time; afterall, why force a college graduation in four years when it could be done in five, seven, or more years. Also, he maintains, black on black violence and murder are also forgiven and not to be feared because of slavery, but such forgiveness should not apply to excessive use of force by police (white or black) nor their unconstitutional acts trying to solve the violence that is to be feared. The approximate 2000 solved murders of "black bodies" by other black bodies and the thousands of other unsolved murders that occur each year are apparently an acceptable price to pay for the American Constitution that is so much of that American "identity" of which he complains.

Though Mr. Coates gives no explicit solution for poverty, he seems to suggest that the only solution is for all non-black Americans — regardless of whether they were ever slaves or slave owners — to pay money to black Americans, either directly or indirectly by means of government welfare, and to provide blacks with their own decent housing, healthcare, and work in which they can enjoy and prosper in their own black identity and culture without fear of Dreamers or the Dream.

In substance, his solution is to establish a separate but equal education system for "black bodies", letting them commit self-genocide by continuing to kill each other, and creating prosperous black ghettos with the help of a new 21st Century slave master: government. We have come full circle. The solution to racism is racism.

G.   Summary

Mr. Coates' advice to his son appears to be: school sucks and life sucks and then you will die and forget about Dreaming because it will not get any better. While this is going on, the Dreamers are out to get you. The Dreamers are people calling themselves white or who happen to be cops though you are more likely to be killed by someone calling themselves black — but there is no such thing as race. If you suffer failure in life or harm others, use slavery as an excuse and pass this excuse down to your descendants. Always remember, I love you. Because of this last piece of advice, I believe the previous may be given with a "wink". What he really intends is to show his son how easy it is to make money dishing out this B.S.; that he is working on a nice trust fund for his son to mess around in college for 5, 7, or whatever years; and to warn him not to mess up such a great gig as Prince Jones did.

It is not the critic who counts; not the man who points out how the strong man stumbles, or where the doer of deeds could have done them better. The credit belongs to the man who is actually in the arena, whose face is marred by dust and sweat and blood; who strives valiantly; who errs, who comes short again and again, because there is no effort without error and shortcoming; but who does actually strive to do the deeds; who knows great enthusiasms, the great devotions; who spends himself in a worthy cause; who at the best knows in the end the triumph of high achievement, and who at the worst, if he fails, at least fails while daring greatly, so that his place shall never be with those cold and timid souls who neither know victory nor defeat.

Theodore Roosevelt

III. BETWEEN THE WORLD AND US

Language, even in its most logical or mathematical form, is a poor expression of empirical realities and incapable of expressing the few absolute truths of life. Even in this simple sentence, you see that I have contradicted myself by telling you in words that it is absolutely true that words cannot express absolute truths. This is the classic "this sentence is false" contradiction and dilemma. I will do the best I can with what language allows to approach nonpragmatic "truth" and hopefully you will continue the battle with the world for truth.

However, language is unambiguously great for lying and for bullshitting.

To great ivory tower thinkers such as Saint Augustine and Kant, lying was a serious moral problem. In real life, everyone lies. By lying, a person at least admits that there is truth out there that needs to be hidden and a lie can empirically be tested — proving a statement false is possible and such proof is what makes a statement scientific.

Bullshitting is worse than any lie. A bull shitter does not care about truth or falsehood but only about achieving intended results. A good bullshit, if done properly by a master of bullshitting, not only cannot be proven false but would be stated in a manner such that whoever hears it does not want to prove it false nor care about whether it is true or false. That is why it is so dangerous and is getting to be more dangerous as we become more of a Technological Society.

A.   The One Undisputed Empirical Truth

Being poor sucks. There is no way around that. Being rich is much better. Getting rich quickly and with little work is the best. One of the few empirical truths of reality has been already summarized by a much better writer than me:

Throughout recorded time, and probably since the end of the Neolithic Age, there have been three kinds of people in the world, the High, the Middle, and the Low. They have been subdivided in many ways, they have borne countless different names, and their relative numbers, as well as their attitude towards one another, have varied from age to age: but the essential structure of society has never altered. Even after enormous upheavals and seemingly irrevocable changes, the same pattern has always reasserted itself, just as a gyroscope will always return to equilibrium, however far it is pushed one way or the other.

The aims of these three groups are entirely irreconcilable. The aim of the High is to remain where they are. The aim of the Middle is to change places with the High. The aim of the Low, when they have an aim -- for it is an abiding characteristic of the Low that they are too much crushed by drudgery to be more than intermittently conscious of anything outside their daily lives -- is to abolish all distinctions and create a society in which all men shall be equal. Thus throughout history a struggle which is the same in its main outlines recurs over and over again. For long periods the High seem to be securely in power, but sooner or later there always comes a moment when they lose either their belief in themselves or their capacity to govern efficiently, or both. They are then overthrown by the Middle, who enlist the Low on their side by pretending to them that they are fighting for liberty and justice. As soon as they have reached their objective, the Middle thrust the Low back into their old position of servitude, and themselves become the High. Presently a new Middle group splits off from one of the other groups, or from both of them, and the struggle begins over again. Of the three groups, only the Low are never even temporarily successful in achieving their aims. It would be an exaggeration to say that throughout history there has been no progress of a material kind. Even today, in a period of decline, the average human being is physically better off than he was a few centuries ago. But no advance in wealth, no softening of manners, no reform or revolution has ever brought human equality a millimeter nearer. From the point of view of the Low, no historic change has ever meant much more than a change in the name of their masters. — George Orwell, <u>1984</u>

Why God so hates the poor that he would create this unbeatable trilogy of life is a mystery that I have spent a lifetime thinking about and am no closer to solving. He is God and can do whatever the fuck he wants. He needs no reason to act. Reason and meaning are human characteristics. God is complete by definition. So why this and not that? I have no clue. In the words of Robert De Niro, "This is this, it is not that, it is this." All I know is that being Low sucks. Anything one can do to avoid it is allowed as long as you can get away with it. One must be smart about it. Getting caught only makes being Low worse. Successful and not successful attempts scar you for life usually both physically and mentally. If you work your way out of the Low legally by self-determination, discipline, and skill without having to sell your soul to the High, it will be by pure luck but most will not be able to admit it and this attitude will scar whatever good they do. If you work out of it illegally or by selling your soul to the High as most do, unless you are a smart, cold-blooded SOB, your victory will be temporary but at least you will be able to pass the victory onto your successors.

Regardless of this permanent Low, it is only the arrogance of the High that would view them as hopeless idiots doomed to a life of misery, drug addiction, violence, and meaningless deaths. Anyone who gives you this impression and claims to be from the Low is lying, these types of lies are big in the United States were having worked from rags to riches is marketed to be a good trait though not treated as such in reality and in which economic class differences and struggles are not acknowledged. There are many spectators and tourists who like to visit the Low temporarily as a break from their boring Middle or High life and then get rich commenting on it.

Although history is usually written as a series of great persons or great minds, history is made by a sum of millions of forever unknown nameless acts by individuals, the vast majority of whom are in forgotten or unmarked graves, and the whole is greater than this sum. The old adage "For Want of A Nail" is not just an admonishment for children. In any detailed reading of history, in every great battle or great event, the difference between glorious victory and inglorious defeat was more often than not a lucky event or fortuitous act of courage by a forever unknown individual. The most important inventions and discoveries in history are by unknowns as are usually the keystones of victories in battle. The millions of Low throughout history have loved and been loved and have struggled and triumphed in every day struggles for life, property, and liberty. They have had happy moments and miserable moments; some had imagination, a strong work ethnic, and intelligence while others had ignorance, laziness, stupidity — whatever emotions and thoughts you have experienced, all humans including the Low have experienced throughout history. The vast majority loved their children and did not intentionally beat them physically or emotionally. In fact the love of the Low for their children was in many ways greater than either the High

56

or Middle could imagine since often the only meaning their lives had was to work for a better life for their children. The vast majority of them were not hopeless drug addicts, criminals, or violent people, even though violence was and had to be a large part of their lives since usually the primary source of their livelihood was physical work that involved violence to their bodies.

Though many had stories about being on top in the "rage of the moment", many others have had more interesting stories about interceding to help a buddy being beaten or facing injustice. Even among the slaves in the Low, the vast majority not only survived with some joy in life, as most slaves throughout history did, but some went on to work their way out of slavery to go on and own their own slaves. The glory and tragedy of human existence are that its greatest qualities only come out in the worse situations and never go on to be publicized or well-known because the High do not want the word to get around nor for these great qualities to become common.

However, though it does not seem possible to improve the essential quality of human nature — call it Original Sin or whatever — much can be done to increase the quantity of joys in this life, and, if you want human life to continue, either as something you owe yourself or to others, much work needs to be done to assure its continuance. Technology and our Technological Society are great and the best ever for this pursuit of happiness and survival. However, they have their problems. In the past, there was necessary cooperation between the High, Middle, and Low to explore, discover, and conquer the world in order to survive. Much of the work of survival took the form of physical work, physical risk, fighting, killing, and dying for survival but at least with the Powers alongside. In the past, the Powers — the Alexander's, Caesar's, Genghis Khan's, and even as most recent as the Napoleon's of the past few centuries of nation building — were expected to fight and risk physical death not only beside you but in the lead.

The technique of power has evolved and no longer has such limitations. Now, sitting warm and cozy in safety from a distance of thousands of miles, the Powers have others do their killing for them and even have machines do their killing in the purest of cold-blooded acts. To the Powers, individuals are simply input data into whatever algorithm they are using to achieve and control power. As bad as the past appears to be in what we perceive as time, at least its destruction of you was meant to be and solely could be physical. As badly as the Powers of the past wanted to destroy any rebellion, opposition, or resistance to their power both physical and in spirit, they were always limited by the available techniques solely to physical destruction of it. King Agamemnon beat Theristes to death for ridiculing the ambition of the Powers, but the ridicule continued and remained as a natural part of the working man's fight and will to survive.

The present technique does not want to allow even such consolation. Our Technological Society is bringing to life O'Brien and his Room 101, but it is not a room with a rat cage but a sterile, pleasantly decorated, warm, friendly room with surround sound of bullshit negating conscious, complex tragedy in the classical sense, to replace it with fear, hatred, and the joy or pain of either triumph or self-abasement loss but no dignity of emotion nor deep or complex sorrow while at the same time denying the truth that 2 + 2 by definition makes four. One of the early critiques and definers of "Technological Society" Jacques Ellul predicted that technology will make liberals arts and all non-machine knowledge useless and meaningless, that the future saints of this new Society will be exemplified by a Steve Jobs, and its new religion will be science. He was wrong on these points. Because technology requires specialization for most, it gives the Powers so much more free time to consciously and knowingly think about and perfect the liberal art of bull shit, power, and control while at the same time being immune to almost all of its bad side effects — the act of collecting and maintaining power is now with those who know nothing else and need no other skill, experience, or knowledge and often are the most ignorant of the technology and machine power over which they have dominion. There are no more saints or devils, only shadowy figures who accept God and power as being one, a demigod the "law", and bullshitters as priests.

Although the Powers still can destroy you physically, the Powers' technique can now destroy you spiritually, which is much worse. It uses fake beatitudes and whatever good exists in human nature not to flower virtues but to make vices appear as the true good. The Powers use racism to foster, spread, and strengthen racism; use claims of caring, empathy, and understanding to foster, spread, and strengthen apathy, enmity, and ignorance. Claims of being a witness and of having experienced injustice, powerlessness, and fear are used by those whose lives were immune to these experiences or who were cowards when faced with it.

I want to provide you with a guide to see through the bullshit. You may not understand what I mean by the "Powers-that-be". Part of me hopes that you always remain ignorant of what I mean and that this writing will always be meaningless to you because this will mean that you are one of them — unlike popular perceptions, going over to the "dark side" is more often than now a guarantee of power, justice, and happiness both in this world and in the next if there is any. If you do understand it, I hope to give you the understanding, will, and means to fight them in a battle that you are destined to lose.

There are common analytical techniques to see through bullshit and to survive it, in order to honorably fight another day. Some are momentary and change as styles or material wealth changes. For example, at present, a man who wears a bow tie is without doubt an asshole and bullshit artist who cannot be trusted. This obviously may change as clothing styles change. There are more universal guides: 1) *ad hominem* analysis and argument is proper; 2) nature including human nature is your enemy, not any individual person; 3) the law is not your friend; 4) morality, ethics, or any attempt to define good and evil cannot be applied to the dead; and 5) accept Despair, including religious Despair.

1. *Ad Hominem*

The Powers often state that they hold nothing personal against those they harm most, it is just business. Even Mr. Coates says that he holds nothing personal against those who call themselves white. This makes practical sense since he seems to be writing to them and wants them to buy his books. Substantively, it is in the nature of the Powers and of bullshit to accuse their opponents of making *ad hominem* arguments as if such are always fallacious or otherwise not sound or invalid. They do this because they have most to fear from proper *ad hominem* argument since they are usually a bunch of hypocrites. (Please remember that accusing someone of being a hypocrite is itself an invalid argument though a good point for moral reasoning. A hypocrite's argument may still be valid but as a hypocrite he should not be making it or passing judgments on others for not accepting it.) You need to know the difference between valid and not valid *ad hominem* argument.

Ad hominem, from the Latin for "to the man" or "to the person", is short for *argumentum ad hominem* and refers to argument attacking the character, motive, or other attribute of the person making the argument, rather than attacking the argument directly. It is a logical fallacy when based solely on some irrelevant fact or supposition about the author or the person being criticized. For example, it is fallacious to argue that Mr. Coates' theory is wrong because his book has a white cover. However, *ad hominem* reasoning is not always fallacious, such as when it relates to the credibility of the speaker or when used in moral reasoning or practical reasoning in which the conclusions are dependent on the speaker having the necessary experience or knowledge. Hopefully, my arguments above on Mr. Coates' premises and reasoning are examples of valid arguments. It is not fallacious to say that Mr. Coates should not be making arguments whose credibility is based on his experience of violence that he has never actually experienced.

You must be very careful with these arguments because bullshitters seem to be natural masters of their intricacies while most people need to think about them to understand them. For example, in response to a certain white person denying an accusation he is racist, the response "he would say that, wouldn't he" is a valid circumstantial *ad hominem* argument. The point being that a man, accused of being a racist, these days at least, would deny the claim whether it was true or false. This argument is valid only insofar as it devalues the denial and does nothing to prove or disprove the accusation because even someone who is not a racist would deny being one. One must usually look to other facts for the truth of such accusations.

More significantly, these arguments are important because they at least admit the existence of the other human against which you are arguing. As I will discuss later, willing "good intentions" may be all you have to call yours in this world but you cannot will "good" without also knowing "evil". Even fallacious *ad hominem* arguments are better, at least from a normative frame of reference if not a pragmatic one, than treating humans as data in an algorithm. At least in making such argument you care enough about them or their existence to hate and ridicule them:

> *The joy of love... the clarity of hatred... the ecstasy of grief. It hurts sometimes more than we can bear. If we could live without passion, maybe we'd know some kind of peace. But we would be hollow. Empty rooms, shuttered and dank. Without passion, we'd be truly dead.*
>
> Angel, <u>Buffy the Vampire Slayer</u>

2.   *Nature*

To say as Mr. Coates says that one knows America as a land acquired through murder is a dishonest, polemic lie that if not based on ignorance not only intentionally hides the truth but diminishes the true extent and power of the heart of darkness that was the reality of the human struggle in the founding of America and that continues to be the reality of human struggle. If such delusional accusations against the past are really accepted or acceptable as explanations for whatever problems one's racial group may be having, such acceptance would be an argument supporting racism and not one against or disproving it.

Columbus and those who followed did not come to a New World Carthage to burn it to the ground, kill its men, enslave its women and children, and then salt the ground to ensure that this thousand year culture would no longer be a pain in its ass. In the absence of any concepts of Christian Divine Law reasoning, they probably should have. As most ancient, pre-Christian states whether republic, empire, Western, Eastern, African, or whatever learned, if someone is not willing to submit, pay you taxes, and offer for service your strongest men and women for your needs and pleasures, then fuck them — crucify them and go on to more important problems. Just as the Roman murder of Carthage was the height of the Roman Republic firmly establishing itself at that time as the undisputable power of the Western World; given their technological advantage, it would have been possible for Spain, France, Britain, or whatever Old World conqueror who came upon the New World to knowingly and intentionally and actually "murder" all of its habitants and not have to deal with the future wars among the New World natives and between so-called native and non-native Americans, nor the future waste of money and time on arguments as to whether naming a fuckin football team "Redskin" is insult or compliment.

Columbus did not bring the concepts of murder nor of slavery to the New World. The Aztec "culture" in their practice of human sacrifice by ripping out the heart of the living and showing it to them quickly while they were still alive perfected murder to an art form beyond the amateurs of Western Civilization. Imagine the Trail of Tears that occurred as Aztec captives were marched in line to Tenochtitlán for their execution by such means. Slavery was an established part of all Central American and South American cultures until they were forced to abandon the practice by their Western conquerors. It was an accepted norm among most of North American Indian life (except for those stuck in Northern free states) until they lost the Civil War — their descendants, as part of their own polemics, have forgotten that most of the American Indian Nations fought in support of the Confederacy and their right to own slaves. The evil white overlords may be responsible for the Middle Passage but not for the enslavement that led to it. The majority were enslaved by their fellow Africans in the same way that they had been for millennia and as they continue to be enslaved today in the last part of the World that still has slavery: Africa. It was mostly Arab Muslim wholesalers who transported the slaves to coastal ports and sold them into the middle link of the Passage.

What Columbus and his followers unknowingly and unintentionally brought to their New World was smallpox, measles, and influenza that resulted in the death of millions in the New World in the same way that these caused the death of millions in the Old World — in the same way the New World's gift of syphilis to the Old World killed millions. Unfortunately, the New World's millions totaled 95% of its population. This was not murder, either by the New World or Old. If you want to call it murder, then its perpetrator is Mother Nature or a still alive God or whatever you want to call the universe and you should be man enough to deal with It or Him instead of cowardly hiding behind accusations of injustices by past dead humans. The truly unfortunate fact about the discovery of the New World by the Old World is that even if Columbus and those who followed came as friends, colleagues, brethren, do-gooders, or whatever instead of as conquerors, given the knowledge of disease at the time, the 95% of the population that died from smallpox, measles, influenza, and the other new diseases still would have died just as the New World syphilis deaths would have still occurred.

If you are truly a compassionate human being and not just pretending to be one, acceptance of this truth should strengthen the Despair caused when one contemplates and empathizes with the human suffering that was part of the establishment of America. It turns out that murder is not simply a human trait that may be done passionately or in cold blood and that only occurs as a choice or when intended; rather, it is an inherent part of both human and non-human nature. Nature gives life and then immediately begins the process of trying to kill it. It is personal, nature is trying to kill you as much as everyone else. It is not just "between the world and me", it is between the world and all of us.

Mr. Coates is wrong when he states that Prometheus hated the birds that tormented him thus he shows his complete misunderstanding of the relationship between life and "nature". Prometheus knew and we must know that the birds are as much victims to the gods' indifference as we are. Prometheus gained his strength and meaning for his life from his hatred of all gods, even a god in the pleasant guise of a "Mother Nature" to hide its indifference to "us." The gods punished Prometheus with an eternity of physical pain, but he was left with his "hate of all gods" to console him and with the knowledge that the power of fire that he gave man remains with them. "To die hating them, that was freedom."

3.   *The Law is not Your Friend*

We can argue whether concepts of morality or ethics have any meaning other than ruling-class ideology, but without doubt, the "law", legal ethics, or whatever an organized society calls its monopoly on violence, including American law, is nothing but ruling-class ideology enforced by a monopoly of violence by its police mercenaries. After being enslaved by law, there is no basis for former slaves or for anyone but the upper class of any society to expect any good from it or from any legal system — just different forms of slavery. For the middle class, it is a necessary evil. For anyone below, it is another evil to be avoided. Given recent "common law" events, I find it difficult to believe that anyone with a minimum of experience and rational analysis of the law — such as just watching television news about it — can think otherwise. Our courts, in their wisdom, and even the majestic Supremes, made up of a politically correct mixture of race and sex — but not poor of course — are causing all sorts of disturbances and fighting among the Middles and Lows, while no one notices that every court in the country in unison has 1) engaged in a mass incarceration of our population never before seen in history or in the world except perhaps for the Stalinist or Maoist Purges; 2) assisted and been keystone to a transfer of wealth and thus power to a small elite not seen since Ancient Egypt; and 3) pretty much destroyed all of the power the working class fought and died to gain during the last century putting economic slavery in its strongest position in American history. It is fitting that while the rest of the world celebrates May 1st as International Workers' Day to commemorate the Haymarket Massacre of 1886 in our very own Chicago — one of the starting points of that century of struggle — we celebrate it as Law Day.

I do not see how anyone can read any history and not come out in complete Despair in the law as a "good". Eliminating discriminatory laws is a good. Creating new laws to replace them, no matter how well intended, always turn bad. Eventually, despite initial success, any new law will come around to bite the Lows and usually most of the Middle. The "law" is what a judge on any particular day says the law is and thus makes the judge for all practical purposes judge, jury, and executioner for the cases before them. Jury trials and bench trials are essentially popularity contests in which the most sympathetic party wins. Appellate decisions are abstract ethical opinions issued by ivory tower ethicists who are not even honest enough to admit what they are and whose underlying facts usually have little or no relationship to what actually happened or is happening.

In our complex Technological Society in America, the average person commits at least three felonies a day without even knowing it. At any time, the law, if it wanted, could find a way to arrest and imprison anyone of us. It does not because it does not want or have a need to do it — yet. The more laws that are created, the more opportunity there is for this luck to run out for all of us. 95% of the American legal system is made up of glorified bookkeepers who issue 6000 to 8000 new laws and regulations every year without accountability to anyone except perhaps to the Powers for whom they work. They survive because they pay the police to enforce their whims, police who are essentially civilian mercenaries organized into legal street gangs. The 5% of lawyers who actually work with a sense of empathy and justice and fight against the Powers live lonely day-to-day lives waiting for the day they will join the ranks of the unemployed or worse.

This Despair should get worse as you move on to contemplate the actual method of the founding of America and the founding of any legal system. Essentially, the process is that barbarians come in, destroy the old legal system, and then create a new one defining themselves as civilized and anyone in opposition as barbarian. America was not tamed by slavery, at least not by slavery as the word is commonly used: slavery as a rule of law. All republics, empires, and states throughout history, at their high and glory, were founded and maintained their power when free men and women risked life, limb, well-being, and fought and died to create and preserve those republics, empires, or states. "Taming" a land by the use of slavery is a sign of decay and the beginning of the end. This was true of all past cultures and was true of American Southern Culture — despite their delusional refusal to admit to it to this day. The end result of slavery in America was not its taming but the Civil

War and its continuing aftershocks that have brought nothing but misery and waste. Not only was the slave's life a degradation of his personal worth but it degraded the society for which he was enslaved.

Then, as now, economic slavery with the aid of slavery as a rule of law was the prevalent technique used to tame a nation. Many of the "free" consisted of legally indentured working-class individuals who, though considered free by the farce that is the law, had nothing to lose in risking life, limb, and well-being in the hope of a better life. Those in economic slavery, that continues to this day and is becoming the norm, often had no better quality of life than the enslaved and often worse.

Who were the founders of America and the writers of the constitutional protections of the law that Mr. Coates and his fellow Highs value so much? It is absolutely true that many were slave owners themselves. You know what else they were? They were tax evaders, pirates, privateers, bootleggers, racketeers, mercenaries, outcastes, anti-social rebels; many were crooks who if ever caught by the British would have been hanged instantly. Their model for the founding of our new nation was neither Athenian democracy nor The City of God but the limited oligarchy of the warrior state of Sparta and perhaps the practical, working democracy of pirate ships. The law-abiding residents at the time of America's founding wanted the status quo, were loyal to the British government, and were afraid of any change as law abiding citizens have always been throughout history regardless of the nature of the government — be it Czarist Russia, Stalinist Russia, North Korea, or whatever form of government happens to be the "law".

In some part, it can be argued that those Founding Rascals failed miserably in their goals but not entirely. This misses the bigger view. Without doubt, the world is quantitatively a better place now than it ever was before it. The American Revolution in itself and in combination with the French Revolution it inspired profoundly altered history, triggered the end of the absolute monarchies that governed the world at the time while replacing them with republics. The revolutionary wars that they unleashed upon the world in the name, hypocritically perhaps, of Christian principles extended from the Caribbean to the Middle East. Regardless of how hypocritical it may seem, putting what were purely philosophical, abstract ideas such as "[w]e hold these truths to be self-evident, that all men are created equal, that they are endowed by their Creator with certain unalienable Rights, that among these are Life, Liberty and the pursuit of Happiness" into a pragmatic, political, government document that was intended to be used and was used as a foundation and form of government was and is revolutionary, and it had occurred previously only in small city-states. Without it all the present apologetics on slavery and race relations would be non-existent: we would still have slaves and slave owners.

The freedoms fostered by these revolutions based on Christian principles have lead to incredible and sudden progress in all of Man's quantitative knowledge: the Industrial Revolution, the scientific revolution, medicine, and every aspect of human endeavor. We live in a world free of smallpox and many of the diseases that literally and actually plagued our predecessors, with treatments for many of the ones that killed off much of the original inhabitants of the New World. We have planes and iron ships and have put men on the Moon. We have invented machines that have changed society quantitatively for the better including radio, television, the internet, and the great invention of internal combustion engines that have allowed for the automobile and the motorcycle — inventions that finally made it possible for even the most parochial of individuals to leave a narrow small village existence to explore, discover, and conquer the world. We have eliminated smallpox and many other diseases from the world. Despite the violence that still exists, by percentage and by quantity, we live in the most non-violent period in history.

4) *Morality, Ethics, or any Attempt to Define Good and Evil cannot be Applied to the Dead*

Much if not all of the above misery was inflicted by Man upon Man through good intentions — God, nature, or whatever one calls reality is what it is, intention is not any part of it. Good and evil are human creations. What we call evil exists in the world because God wants it to exist — it is not good or evil to Him, it just is. Intention is the sign of an incomplete or imperfect being because it needs or wants something other than itself. God by definition is complete and perfect and does not need or want anything. He is God, He can do whatever the fuck He wants. He brought you into this world and can take you out anytime and any way He wants. If you have a problem with that, take it up with the Living God and not with your dead ancestors. "Good intention" is not only "a hall pass through history" for the dead as Mr. Coates accurately states for once, it might be the only freedom that Mankind has. It might well be that we live in a completely deterministic universe in which what we perceive as time and space are really one big donut in which everything that was ever done, is done, or will be done, is fixed and determined and simply repeats once it circles back. In that case, as great philosophers such as Spinosa have pointed out, your only freedom is the knowledge that you are not free and what you do with that knowledge. Accept it or fight hopelessly against it? Descartes was wrong, it is not "I think, therefore I am", it is "I am, therefore I think". Your intentions, good or bad, may be all you have.

Our ancestors, of all races, creeds, ethnicities, and sexes fought against their destiny to face battles, dangers, and harms that most of the modern apologetics for and against racism and fear can barely comprehend and most of the time are too lazy to even try comprehending. Instead of giving in to fear and staying within the shelter of small villages and even small cities — relative to us — in which they could have lived their whole lives, they fanned out throughout the globe without the aid of modern navigation, communications, medicine, science, or our extensive empirical knowledge usually by walking or at best upon animals or wooden ships all the while suffering disease, hunger, starvation, fights, and death at the hand of other travelers, and of course enslavement by these other travelers. They faced the exact same Despair that we face under worse physical suffering, rejected it, and opened their hearts "to the benign indifference of the universe" to give it meaning, to make a difference, or create love and hate in this life because without Despair of life there is neither.

The Powers want us to believe that this quantitative improvement is the result of great individual minds, from a Thomas Jefferson or a John Locke to a Max Planck or Albert Einstein. This is bullshit. Most of the great scientific discoveries of the modern world are a result of luck, both empirically and theoretically. None of these great minds would be anything if they had not been born in a world that allowed for their work to prosper and their ideas to be accepted, in a world created by the struggles and "good intentions" of millions of unknown souls. The words, "the living, rather, to be dedicated here to the unfinished work which they who fought here, have, thus far, so nobly advanced" should not be taken to refer only to the Honored Dead who fought and died at Gettysburg but to all of those who struggled in life with good intentions as we should be doing. To use their struggles as a whining excuse for present injustices or to reject them as failed, immoral Dreamers and their failed "good intentions" as worthless Dreams is to accept the meaningless of life and to reject the struggle that is human life. One Despairs more from the past when one realizes how many unknown persons in history have contributed to the present — the most forgotten appear to be those who acted with the most "good intentions."

Qualitatively, living Mankind appears to be no better now that it ever was or will be. This is not a judgment that neither should nor can rationally apply to the past. Even assuming that concepts of morality or ethics have a meaning other than ruling-class ideology, which is doubtful, it is only the arrogance of the Powers that allows them to apply it to the past. Ethical theories and moral theories apply to living people in the present, though they may be based on concerns for the future. Our past dead ancestors are not moral, immoral, amoral, or ethical or unethical, they are dead.

Until recent history, slavery was not "criminal", it was legal with the Powers as usual gaining the most from it.

Moral judgments of the dead are usually made by hypocrites who would have done no better. Saying that one does not want to be and should not expected to be a martyr while at the same time ranting against the "machinery of criminal power" and "criminal irresponsibility" of past humanity denotes both arrogance and irresponsibility. Mr. Coates writes that he witnessed the events of "9/11" from his Brooklyn rooftop and his emotional response was: "[b]ut looking out upon the ruins of America, my heart was cold. I had disasters all of my own. ... In the days after, I watched a ridiculous pageantry of flags, the machismo of firemen, the overwrought slogans. ... I could see no difference between the officer who killed Prince Jones and the police who died, or the firefighters who died". If you are witness to 3500 lives being snuffed out in a moment, you essentially have three options: 1) laugh at it as many combat veterans do in order to deal with the pain; 2) cry out with pain and look for relief through slogans, machismo, or whatever; 3) not give a fuck. If you pick the third option, you cannot say that you do not give a fuck now but would have given a fuck one hundred and fifty years ago if you witnessed some lives unjustly killed back then. If you do not give a fuck now, it is doubtful you would have in the past. It is easy to love "humanity" but very difficult to love humans. Modern apologetics for the Powers criticize the past for not doing better though it is a certainty that given the same facts they would have not done any better.

Watch out for hypocrites such as Mr. Coates who calmly talk about how violence was part of their family and community; explain how it is an excuse or justification for any present violent acts they may have made or will make; boast of their sexual exploits in college as a learning experience; talk of heroes such as Malcolm X as preachers of truth despite his life and death disproving that truth; and talk peace while naming their children not only after warriors but after failed warriors.

Most of all watch out for those hypocrites who spit out bullshit about having rejected magic, dogma, and our "goal-oriented" era, so that they can deal solely with how to live as an individual. History has firmly established that these hypocrites and their self-centered view of reality when given the opportunity and need will cold-bloodedly kill you and anything associated with you. Though such sycophants live and have lived their whole lives in a relatively free and healthy world, they claim that both they and their family and community have turned to violence and hate because of past slavery inflicted by others' past dead ancestors on their dead ancestors. If such cause and effect actually exists, then how would these poor souls at the mercy of past harms have acted if the harm were actual and real: would they have martyred themselves instead of enslaving their fellow humans as was legal and expected like everyone else; would they have martyred themselves instead of grasping the opportunity and risks of working as a sailor on a slaveship; in the prime of their manly youth, would they have enlisted to join military expeditions against slavers, abolitionists, or underground railroads at risk of losing valuable learning experience with their girlfriends? Most certainly not. At best, they would have done what they do now: enjoy the pleasures of life as spectators of the human struggle around them and then get rich commenting and criticizing it in the manner expected by the Powers. They would have no more acted to stop the now entitled "criminal" acts of the past then they do now.

In the past, as now, humanity developed ways to survive in life, in or out of slavery, prison, or in whatever miserable condition they found themselves though most of it was delusional, as most Dreams are, but this did not stop them from Dreaming. In or out of slavery, many — likely most since perfectly functioning families are rare — came from dysfunctional families but dreamed of having a family; many found little love in life but dreamed of love; and most had no formal education but dreamed of an education for their children. To be a man, in or out of slavery, you were expected to marry and to support your children, both "free" love and adoration of violence were left to bandits running around in the jungle, regardless of any excuses you may have.

I remember my father coming home one day from his construction laborer job and describing how two of his co-workers died that day buried alive in a ditch collapse. He went to work the next day. I also remember him taking every opportunity upon any injury to collect workers' compensation or whatever free money he could get. I remember him on a bad day taking it out on my mother by beating her. I also remember becoming at least half-a-man when I put a stop to it. Even though most of my life is a vague haze, there are so many good and bad stories to tell about my boring childhood in Cicero that they could fill up multiple books. The same would be true of your grandparents who survived World War II and a communist revolution to make it to the United States as Dreamers hoping the Dream. The lives of the poor including of slaves are as rich emotionally, rationally, and physically as of any of the High except for one thing: they were materially poor with no idea or illusion of power to control their lives — they went as the dialectic of history went and they knew it. It may be true that we all lead pre-determined lives but the High and usually part of the Middle, such as the intelligentsia, have the power to recognize it and with that power comes freedom. However there is no basis to assume the poor, enslaved or not, lack the experience or the capability to experience the full range of human will and reason.

<u>5) *Accept Despair, including Religious Despair to go Beyond It*</u>

There is no love of life without despair of life.
— Albert Camus

As my essay so far should show to you, anything approaching the truth is usually much worse than bullshit. This is a common characteristic of bullshit. If it were to make things appear as bad as they are or as good as it is, it loses its power by either leaving no room for hope or no need for it. It needs hope to keep its power. The world that is between Mr. Coates and him is much worse that he describes; if he is in fear now, he would be in greater fear if he actually bothered to search for truth. This is the despairing truth of reality for you but also is its glory as the working class hero Albert Camus has shown because it beats the world of fear that Mr. Coates and his fellow pundits propagate and that seems now to be the soul of America. "But in the end one needs more courage to live than to kill himself." *Albert Camus*.

Finally, I want to deal with Despair and religion. To many, apparently including Mr. Coates, religion is the ultimate lie. To others it is the ultimate truth. To simply ignore it or to deal with it polemically without sincere, deep, and thoughtful analysis based both on historical fact and personal experience is bullshit. It is something that cannot be avoided in any analysis of modern bullshit or the modern Technological Society. The answer to the question of "why is there something instead of nothing" is one's god. If someone is conscious, this question is ever present. The substance of consciousness is probably the asking of this question and running into nothing but obstacles to get an answer. Our will wants an answer. The answer depends on whether you can withstand Despair to go beyond it and whether you view the world as between it and "me" or as between you and "us".

Truth should not only make you a cynic, as Mr. Coates claims he avoids, but should make you go beyond cynicism to Despair. Part of me hopes that you always remain ignorant of what I mean by Despair, that you will never have to make the choice to survive it, and that this part of my writing will always be meaningless to you as the earlier parts would be. If you do understand it, I hope you have the understanding, will, and means to fight and win this battle despite the simultaneous battle against the Powers that you are destined to lose — if you decide to fight that battle. Though having excuses such as past racism upon which to blame the injustices of one's life avoids destructive Despair, it also stops you from making the leap of will to see life not as a delusion of being "between the world and me" but of the more difficult and challenging real battle "between the world and us". When such excuses are fostered and propagated by those same Powers-that-be, they do so as a temptation for you to succumb to their racism, sexism, or whatever -ism is the latest fad disguised as compassion serving to weaken you and thus strengthen them. Despair should be a source of strength not fear and weakness.

If you choose or are chosen to accept life in Despair, do it as Camus describes, honestly and passionately even though you have limited practical options on how to live it. Do not say that you do not know if God exists or that he does not exist, say you do not care whether He exists or not. There is great individual power in such a life having no rules of morality, ethics, or whatever the Powers call their most recent ideology to keep everyone in check. "Integrity has no need of rules." "'Everything is permitted' is not an outburst of relief or of joy, but rather a bitter acknowledgment of a fact." Camus' existentialist heros are the Don Juan, as "[t]here is no noble love but that which recognizes itself to be both short-lived and exceptional"; the actor, who "demonstrates to what degree appearing creates being", and "[i]n those three hours he travels the whole course of the dead-end path that the man in the audience takes a lifetime to cover"; and the conqueror warrior who waives all promises of eternity to engage in human history, choosing action over contemplation yet constantly aware that nothing can last and no victory is final.

If Mr. Coates truly believes that "the spirit and soul are the body and brain, which are destructible" then he has no basis to complain about others, including past dead others, who gave priority to the happiness of their own body and brain over those of others including those of their slaves. If you are going to subsume Christian Virtues into your existentialism, as Camus accurately pointed out, you are not an existentialist. If you are going to subsume them into a claim of atheism, agnosticism, or whatever, you are also not an existentialist but dishonest and a coward.

But what if you want more out of life? Though Camus' existentialist life has integrity, it involves dishonesty toward one important fact: they are not alone. Again, it is not the world and me, it is the world and us. The "I" of "I am, therefore I think" has no meaning absent a multiplicity of other "I's". A solipsist cannot exist because he would not know it if he did; if "me" really is and makes up all being, there would be no way to be conscious of it. What if I want to experience and know these other "I's" in the same way that I would want them to experience me? As the philosopher Harry G. Frankfurt has written in his book entitled "Truth":

> We learn that we are separate beings in the world, distinct from what is other than ourselves, by coming up against obstacles to the fulfillment of our intentions - - that is, by running into opposition to the implementation of our will. When certain aspects of our experience fail to submit to our wishes, when they are on the contrary unyielding and even hostile to our interests, it then becomes clear to us that they are not parts of ourselves. We recognize that they are not under our direct and immediate control; instead, it becomes apparent that they are

independent of us. That is the origin of our concept of reality, which is essentially a concept of what limits us, of what we cannot author or control by the mere movement of our will.

To the extent that we learn in greater detail how we are limited, and what the limits of our limitation are, we come thereby to delineate our own boundaries and thus to discern our own shape. We learn what we can and cannot do, and the sorts of efforts we must make in order to accomplish what is actually possible for us. We learn our powers and our vulnerabilities. This not only provides us with an even more emphatic sense of our separateness. It defines for us the specific sort of being that we are.

Camus' existentialists are unable to convert their life philosophy of living an individual life to a living society — at least not one in which slavery and racism are wrongs. *The Plague* was an attempt, but living under the stress of plague as a means of building a functioning society is no different than living under the threat of war. It provides a means for a social consciousness to go beyond just the living and the dead, to define heroes, cowards, good, and evil, but not a normative basis on which to avoid slavery, racism, or anything other than to deal with purely pragmatic concerns — which is what I admire about the pre-Christian era. When the Roman Senate or the Athenian democracy discussed and argued about whether to commit what we now call genocide or to enslave a conquered people, they were honest enough to view it solely as pragmatic concerns in difficult times: can we use these people in the future as allies or is it better to use them as examples? They were not bothered with concepts such as all men being made in God's image or any of the formerly Christian but now publicly accepted, in least in the United States for now, normative principles that cause society problems when we try to deal with life.

Whether fortunate or not, if you want to "[lay your] heart open to the benign indifference of the universe" and do more than create an individual who is honest and sincere to its indifference but want to create a society that acknowledges individuals living in its indifference in which slavery and its related evils are wrongs while also having the strength and cohesion to take on nature and discover, explore, and conquer it, then more is required than acceptance of Despair and the individual will to survive it. There must be a social or community will to survive it. To create this social purpose, you as an individual must spit in the face of Despair and move on to creating a difference. You must move from Sisyphus to Prometheus and give Man fire. In religion's case, the fire consists of hope.

Karl Marx may be right that religion is the opium of the people, but so what? Especially for the poor stuck in a never-ending battle with everyone else. If a disease is incurable, a doctor is not wrong to give a patient opium to relieve the pain and provide a quiet death if the patient asks for it. Only rich people would say that they want to be one with nature and its pain because they know that at any moment, if they change their mind, they can get whatever drugs or delusions they want to numb the pain. This is not true for most of humanity. I find it fitting that the first existentialist thinkers were Christians especially the most prolific on this issue: Søren Kierkegaard.

All Christian theology rejects Pascal's Gamble as a valid proof for the existence of a Christian God, as they mostly do with existentialist thought such as Kierkegaard. I have never understood why. As some of my Navy shipmates would say, reality is for people who cannot handle drugs. Life sucks and then you die, so why live in delusional fear or the "absurd" life of an existentialist hero when you can have hope through a leap of hope or faith as Kierkegaard would call it? Why not join the multiples of "I's" who have lived and died through time to make you what you are today as an "us" not just a bullshit "me"?

There is no more irrational debate in our Technological Society than on the subject of religion, except maybe for war. The amount of false advertizing and marketing spent for and against it is dwarfed, maybe, only by the amount spent on war. A study of religion requires real thought and historical research. We have to read both sides and then apply your life experience to read between the lines to get anywhere close to the truth. Religion, in its various forms, always was and is the dominant technique used to understand nature and organize society, from the ancient worship of the state and its leaders as gods to the divine right of kings to the present worship of statistical algorithms as a demigod. The majority of lives are born into their religion, but thanks to our modern Technological Society, you and most Americans now have the option to approach it rationally. Ultimately, however, your choice of religion — a choice everyone makes including atheists and agnostics — is an act of will not reason if it is an act at all.

Is it possible for an individual to reject Christianity and pretend to reject the existence of a god and still lead a good and noble life in whatever conditions? Yes. In fact, most good people who have lived and are living are not Christians. Paraphrasing Camus, most "people expend tremendous energy merely to be normal." As I told you above, you cannot change the lives of the dead or the lives of most living people. The question you face if you decide or are allowed to go beyond individual Despair is how do you individually battle for a society whose normative principles prohibit slavery, racism, and associated evils. The question for you now is how do you give meaning to the words "good" and "evil."

As I have always told you, the ontological proof is the only sound, valid, and irrefutable proof for the existence of God, but it is pretty much worthless. The God it proves exists as Mr. Coates accurately describes: "has no respect for us. It has no use for us ... [I]ts vengeance is not the fire in the cities but the fires in the sky." It proves the existence of a God that would create a world in which He bestows power on a few and leaves most of humanity to suffer as their playthings. Of course, it is His world; He can do whatever He wants with it, but such truth does not make it any easier to live it. The real issue is whether there exists a loving or comforting God that Christianity states there is. The only purpose the proof serves is to prove wrong atheist and agnostic arguments that their positions are the only rational choice. In the end, it does not really do that either because in the end the means out of Despair of religion is not reason but an act of will.

I have never met an atheist or agnostic who substantively believes in their position on God, either the Christian God or just God, though they work hard on appearances. If they really did, they would be existentialist with better things to do than to rationalize their conclusions, give themselves names, or create nominal normative principles by which to guide their life or society. One of the side effects of our Technological Society, thanks to science and related technique, is that it has given us great power, at least temporarily, over nature. As I said at the beginning of this essay, the lucky Powers who enjoy the power of our Technological Society are no longer expected to work for it, fight for it, or do anything but generate the bullshit that is necessary to get and keep this power. It is easy for them to claim atheism or agnosticism and then subsume into it Christian virtues and act as if the virtues are natural to them and to the making of a society. They are never tested on this subsuming and likely never will be. Without exception, those who bother to call themselves atheist or agnostic not only do believe in a god but usually a comforting version of a god. The vast majority cowardly and dishonestly subsume the Christian God into their delusion, most without a clue as to what they are doing.

The most common comforting version of a secular god or demigod worshiped by atheists and agnostics is one's self. In practice, this comes out as a Master Morality as described by Nietzsche but I do not use these words derogatorily as so many people do. Masters in normal situations often times enjoy the seven heavenly virtues as well as the seven deadly sins. In practice, it is hard to tell the difference between the followers of this demigod from any other. It comes up only through individual cross examination of a person or in rare tests of pure empathy — something people rarely allow — that would reveal whether they really see life as being between the world and us or just their "me". In addition, since people change, there is no assurance that a self-demigod of today will also be a person's demigod of tomorrow nor that people will be honest about what god they worship. The same is true for the existentialist; individual identity often changes in the moment. The Master Morality of the Nazis probably cost them World War II, but it has won many battles and other wars for its adherents and will in the future, as it is doing now. The Master Morality is the religion of the Powers and serves them well, but it has believers in all aspects of humanity, including among the Middle and Lows. If you find the lowest group of humans with the lowest standard of living and almost no material wealth or any type of power, I guarantee you that there will be those who manage and delegate what little power there is based on "me".

Making oneself the alpha and the omega of being is very comforting and empowering. In many ways, I envy them. Most will have more friends, loves, and accolades than I could even imagine in my absurd world. They will have virtues and vices like everyone else and usually are the survivors of any bad situation. As Mr. Coates advises his son, being a martyr is for fools. However, though they pretend they can simply assume Christian values, you cannot build a society of freedom in which slavery and racism are "evils" if "me" and my personal identity, views, opinions, and beliefs are the keystone of all life. When this Master Morality runs into another morality that disagrees with it, it has no basis by which to rationally argue against it — it becomes a pure, pragmatic issue of force as with the ancients: there is no God's image or equality of all humans problem that gives value to obstacles consisting of another humans in my pursuit of happiness.

Next we have the in-between demi-gods who vary from place to place and time and culture. In American culture, the most common are the comforting demigods of law, nature, and science. I have already told you about the nature of the law, but its nature does not destroy the comforting nature of this demi-god to its delusional adherents. At least law has a normative basis upon which to build a society, one that favors the Powers. The law giveth and the law taketh it away. Be it North Korea or the Republic of San Marino, the law will support and try to make their Powers prosper. Worshiping nature is equivalent to a woman worshiping someone trying to rape her or a man worshiping someone trying to murder him. I guess it is possible, but it would not survive living outside of caves and would not get society anywhere near discovery, exploration, and conquering the universe. These two demi-gods are truly for the deluded and not worth further analysis of them. If one actually reads and studies history, these demi-gods will do a good job of ridiculing themselves.

Science is a relatively new demigod but probably one of the best to those who are not actually scientists, which I find very funny. Aristotle and Isaac Newton were closer to a unified theory of everything than modern physicists are or inherently can be given the contradictions between various scientific fields of study that they try to avoid by simply ignoring and by their own principles that they cannot ignore such as Godel's Incompleteness Theorems, Heisenberg's Uncertainty Principle, and Bell's Theorem. Richard Dawkins can delude himself and write as many books as he wants about the "God Delusion" but worshiping statistical analysis because it gives you a high probability of being right until it is not right simply because you give it a fancy name such as Quantum Mechanics is just another religion and demigod and worse than most. Science is the art of coming up with statements that can be proven false by experiment. Because they can be proven false does not logically nor practically make them an answer to the question of why there is something instead of nothing that must by necessity involve a proven truth. A majority of mathematicians are Platonist. Some of the greatest logical minds of the 20 Century were also Platonist, such as Kurt Godel and Sir Roger Penrose. Essentially these great minds were numerologists, though I doubt they would admit to such a Pythagorean religion. Einstein studied physics because "I want to know God's thoughts; the rest are details." In Einstein's creed entitled "What I Believe," he wrote at the conclusion: "To sense that behind everything that can be experienced there is something that our minds cannot grasp, whose beauty and sublimity reach us only indirectly: this is religiousness. In this sense ... I am a devoutly religious man." In response to Einstein's criticism of Quantum Mechanics that "I am convinced that He (God) does not play dice", Bohr responded "Einstein, don't tell God what to do"; these do not sound like minds that have given up on the concept of God.

These are sound bites that I give you solely to incite your interest in the beauty of modern science and the simple foolishness of calling it the end of God. Master Morality may be the end of God but not a bunch of tautologies that are too complex to us but would be simple to a mind that was great enough to compute them and that by their own definition are incomplete and uncertain. If God is dead, make it so by willing it, do not wimp out by pretending a bunch of scientists looking for God did it for you.

I love science and technology so much that I worry that its worship by non-scientists and delusional hypocrites like Dawkins may some day in the near future be its downfall. We need it in order to go on discovering, exploring, and conquering the universe. It is easy to worship it now in its infancy because of all the success it is having. Eventually, as with all prior epic changes in human history, it will meet its match in some form as it goes into its teenage years and adulthood, and then these fair-weather believers will abandon it for another god. I do not want to lose it to these hypocrites nor should you. Science and technology have given the poor the best quantitatively measured lives in their history. In America, the poor have access to material wealth and health that was rare even for the rich a century earlier — such as no slavery. All wealth and quantitative wealth are relative. For their lives to continue to get better, science and the social normative principles to keep it going are necessary. Fuck the rich, they will always have wealth.

It is important to remember that modern science developed as an offspring of Medieval Christian Theology's emphasis on reason's ability to understand God independently of revealed dogma. Do not listen to that crap about the Christian Church as being against science and reason, into which they always throw in false stories about Galileo. Galileo was not punished because he theorized that the Earth revolved around the Sun, he was punished because he said that such was true based solely on his authority and intuition, despite the fact that he had no proof of it. He was putting the authority of his individual mind and intuition above knowledge provided by God as far as the Church was concerned, and, the reality is, we now know the Church was right according to modern General Relativity Theory. We now know that time/space is relative. The Earth moving around the sun is a mathematically simpler version of this relative motion, but there is no such thing as absolute or non-relative motion of one body around another. If a mind could handle the mathematical complexity of such a model, it would be able to construe a model of everything revolving around the Earth.

Do not listen to the masters who casually dismiss religion on the basis of their casual knowledge of science. The day will come when they will do the same for science. I do not know what their new demigod will be at that point except that it will be based on a Master Morality and trying to imagine it is one thing that puts me in fear for you and for Mr. Coates' son and for all future generations. It might make the ovens of World War II that killed Jews, Christians, communists, rebels, unionists, and all adherents of a Slave Morality equally and efficiently pale in comparison; it might not only physically kill but also kill Man's soul, including his ability and willingness to accept and live past Despair:

> *We'll be fighting in the streets*
> *With our children at our feet*
> *And the morals that they worship will be gone*
> *And the men who spurred us on*
> *Sit in judgement of all wrong*

They decide and the shotgun sings the song

"Won't Get Fooled Again"   <u>The Who</u>

All other religions, including Islam and Judaism, emphasize and place justice and compliance with its laws above reason. According to them, there is no rational knowledge of God but only revealed knowledge through His given laws. Science developed, was sponsored, and is the long term result of Christian theology. For science to continue when the time comes for its present fair weather worshipers to abandon it, it will need the hope that is the fire provided by Christianity: that reason independent of revealed dogma can know "God's thoughts."

Finally, there is the comfortable gods of the old school religions and the comfortable and loving God of Christianity. My writing on this is fairly silly given the Christian theological concept of Predestination, which I also find irrefutable. If God wants you to believe in Him or in certain demigods or not, you will. I write this essay to you anyway because regardless of what you end up believing or not believing, it is important that you know that knowledge of it is freedom. The only rational proof of the Christian God is Pascal's Wager that all Christian theology rejects. I do not understand why, especially these days when we are willing to bet our world on the wagers of Quantum Mechanics. It is their theology, obviously my opinion means nothing. Kierkegaard's Leap of Faith is not a proof, but it does seem to be taken more seriously by Christian theologians. Whatever, I am concerned with a pragmatic choice. We are looking for a basis beyond Despair and beyond a view of the world as a struggle solely between it and "me" to a foundation for society in which racism and slavery can be defined as "evils".

It is irrational and pragmatically dishonest to treat all religions as equals, especially to equate a warrior religion such as Islam with a Slave Morality such as Christianity, unless you assume a Master Morality with you as the beginning and end of it. If you care about the many that make up the "I" of "I am, therefore I think", all religions are not equal especially when viewed on the basis of good intentions that may be the only free basis by which you have to judge them. The prophet Mohammed came out of his 40 days of meditation and temptation in the dessert to start an army, militarily conquer the Middle East and parts of North Africa, build a great commercial empire, and die one of the richest men in the world. Christianity's hero Jesus Christ came out of 40 days in the dessert to die poor, alone, and as a criminal. This is the difference between a Master Morality and a Slave Morality.

Only those who are ignorant of history ignore the pragmatic effect of this difference of founders upon human history as Christianity developed through time. Without doubt, as any theologian will tell you, the birth of Jesus Christ needed the *Pax Romana* for its timing. It needed the peace provided by that military empire and its roads, which all led to Rome to flourish and spread. As with all things human, Christianity has in it all aspects of our human nature that causes us Despair. After this founding that gave the world the Beatitudes, also without doubt, it went on to give "us" the normative principles for a government and society that rejects slavery and racism, not on purely pragmatic considerations, but as a normative principle of governance. Whether it will continue to be the foundation of such normative principles or whether it and these principles will eventually be lost as just another bump in the road for the advancing power of the Powers-that-be remains to be seen. This uncertainty remains my only and worse fear for you.

The key to picking a religion should also be on how it deals with the fact that God hates the poor and loves the powerful. Christianity deals with this issue by creating a Trinity. In Christianity, God realizes the problem of His nature and so becomes Jesus Christ to show His love for humanity, with their relationship being the Holy Spirit. "In the beginning was the *logos*, and the *logos* was with God, and the *logos* was God." This is a substantial and keystone dogma of Christianity that associates its founder Jesus Christ with the Greek *"logos"*, that is, "word", "discourse", or "reason", i.e., rationality or reasoning. This is the same word from which we derive "logic". This is the name or title of Jesus Christ, seen in Christianity as the pre-existent Second Person of a Trinitarian God.

Modern masters ridicule these beliefs while at the same time, at least for now, casually assume as true popular beliefs that are just as far-fetched to our rational intuition, as pointed out even by the scientific founders of such beliefs such as Werner Heisenberg: light that is both a wave and a particle at the same time, electrons, neutrons, protons, Quantum Mechanics, dark matter, entropy, and all sorts of contradictory mathematical fictions that no one can see, hear, or experience and by definition no one can see, hear, or experience. They accept these because mathematical predictions can be made using them that can be proven false: that is they pragmatically work. There is no reason not to accept Christianity on the same basis: it works to create forms of government that bar slavery and racism and tries to put into real world government and working society Christian Virtues and the Beatitudes. In the end, they will not be successful as nothing we do will be successful to beat the Powers but they work better than anything else found so far. If you want to beat Despair and fight a good fight in the battle between the world and "us", this is the best means of doing it.

This Trinity is an interesting and new way of approaching the problem of the nature of God that I do not see addressed in any way by other religions. If you choose to follow it, I will leave it to the theologians to guide you through but you should not mention this pragmatic approach to Christianity. Taking a pragmatic view of Christianity in the same way that Pascal did and maybe that Kierkegaard did may be rejected by theologians but fuck them. As far as I can see, theologians spend way too much time with the Powers than they do with working class heros.

IV. SUMMARY

I hope that you will never need this essay, except perhaps in so far as it serves as an example of how to see through bullshit by analysis using reason and an honest application of life experience and history to people's assertions about life. You may not even need it for that purpose if you are a bullshit artist yourself. Mr. Coates and his kind will succeed in life much better than anyone such as me or anyone who reaches Despair and fights through it to viewing the world passionately and with empathy as a battle between it and "us"; except they will live life in fear and without ever knowing the happiness of "liv[ing] to the point of tears."

If you can keep your head when all about you
  Are losing theirs and blaming it on you,
If you can trust yourself when all men doubt you,
  But make allowance for their doubting too;
If you can wait and not be tired by waiting,
  Or being lied about, don't deal in lies,
Or being hated, don't give way to hating,
  And yet don't look too good, nor talk too wise:

If you can dream—and not make dreams your master;
  If you can think—and not make thoughts your aim;
If you can meet with Triumph and Disaster
  And treat those two impostors just the same;
If you can bear to hear the truth you've spoken
  Twisted by knaves to make a trap for fools,
Or watch the things you gave your life to, broken,
  And stoop and build 'em up with worn-out tools:

If you can make one heap of all your winnings
  And risk it on one turn of pitch-and-toss,
And lose, and start again at your beginnings
  And never breathe a word about your loss;
If you can force your heart and nerve and sinew
  To serve your turn long after they are gone,
And so hold on when there is nothing in you
  Except the Will which says to them: "Hold on!"

If you can talk with crowds and keep your virtue,
  Or walk with Kings—nor lose the common touch,
If neither foes nor loving friends can hurt you,
  If all men count with you, but none too much;

If you can fill the unforgiving minute
  With sixty seconds' worth of distance run,
Yours is the Earth and everything that's in it,
  And—which is more—you'll be a Man, my son.

If
Rudyard Kipling

Elegies Written in a Country Churchyard:

"Cambridge, a Negor boy belonging to Robert Oliver, Esq. aged 3 years He died Dec. 14 1747"
"Betty, a Negro Servant of Col. Robert Oliver, Died Feb 19 1748 aged about 25 years"
"Bristol, a Negro Servant of Mr. John Foster Died June 24 1748 aged about 30 years old"
> — three graves grouped together in the Dorchester North Burying Ground, Massachusetts.

"In memory of the soldiers of the revolution Who died during the siege of Boston And were buried in this lot"
> — gravestone marking the mass grave of 40 unknown soldiers of the American Revolutionary War grouped together in the Dorchester North Burying Ground, Massachusetts.

President Lincoln delivered the Gettysburg Address on 19 November 1863 on the Gettysburg Battlefield:

Fourscore and seven years ago our fathers brought forth, on this continent, a new nation, conceived in liberty, and dedicated to the proposition that all men are created equal. Now we are engaged in a great civil war, testing whether that nation, or any nation so conceived, and so dedicated, can long endure. We are met on a great battle-field of that war. We have come to dedicate a portion of that field, as a final resting-place for those who here gave their lives, that that nation might live. It is altogether fitting and proper that we should do this. But, in a larger sense, we cannot dedicate, we cannot consecrate—we cannot hallow—this ground. The brave men, living and dead, who struggled here, have consecrated it far above our poor power to add or detract. The world will little note, nor long remember what we say here, but it can never forget what they did here. It is for us the living, rather, to be dedicated here to the unfinished work which they who fought here have thus far so nobly advanced. It is rather for us to be here dedicated to the great task remaining before us—that from these honored dead we take increased devotion to that cause for which they here gave the last full measure of devotion—that we here highly resolve that these dead shall not have died in vain—that this nation, under God, shall have a new birth of freedom, and that government of the people, by the people, for the people, shall not perish from the earth.

About the backcover:

The backcover logo is for the *Knights of Thermopylae Inn of Court,* a non-profit whose resources were used for the writing of this book.

www.betweenworldandus.com

www.sandpebblespodcast.com